Serenity
in
Sandy Shoes

Lyric Poetry for
Reading at
the Shore

Doris Dix Caruso

Seashore Journals

Graham, North Carolina

Grateful acknowledgement is given to the following publications in which certain of these poems have appeared:

Getting Married: a planning magazine
Chicago, Illinois

The Lyricist: the literary magazine of
Campbell University,
Buies Creek, North Carolina

Bay Leaves: The Poetry Council of North Carolina
Annual Edition

Published by   **SEASHORE JOURNALS**
146 West Crescent Square Drive,
Graham, North Carolina, 27253

Revised
Third Edition 2004

ISBN 1-57502-497-7

Printed in the USA by
HARLAN

PUBLISHING
P.O. Box 397 ~ Summerfield, North Carolina ~ (336) 643-5849

CONTENTS

I. SANDY SHOES

II. WINGS

III. SOUNDINGS

IV. SANDCASTLES

For everyone who has ever
experienced peace and renewal
just by sitting on a beach,
any beach!

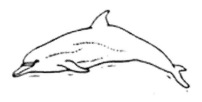

"By words the mind is winged."

—Aristophanes (450-385 B.C.)

SANDY SHOES

Best wishes –
July 2008

Doris Dix Caruso

SANDY SHOES

If I were asked, and I could choose,
I'd walk again in sandy shoes
across a dune and down the beach
to where the white gulls swoop and screech,
to sea oats waving in warm airs
on hermit crabs with vacant stares
to waves of salt and spume and spray,
to porpoises that dance all day…

If I were asked and I could choose,
I'd walk again in Sandy Shoes.

BEACH

A place to walk – a windy, lonesome place

Prevailing wind – offshore – with twilight
              nearly gone – nearly gone

and now the stones beneath my feet feel sharper.

SHIPWRECK — Cape Point, 1972

The date long lost
when her keel was laid,
her timbers rotted,
her planks decayed:
She stands still proud
on the dry blown sand
yet longs for the days
she was free of land,
free under sail
in the open sky,
prow moving tall,
spume dashing high.

Now she must sit
land- locked till the end
as the seagull passes
and greets his friend.

ESSENCE OF THE "BANKS"

Believe these islands, splashed
                    in constant sun
permit wild, restless birds to
                    swoop and soar.

Believe this hidden paradise begun
on timeless beach and faithful to the roar
    of infinite ocean building to a tide,
then pounding, pulling all our senses bare
    esteems we pour such happiness inside…

… to find enchantment waiting for us there.

HOLY PLACE

I find no holier place
    than on a beach,
For here I sit content
    as waters reach
in endless vision of the
    sea and sky,
making me conscious of
    how small am I.

The daily contest of life's
    worldly woe
here is erased with each
    wave's ebb and flow;
so loosed from garish colors
    where men trod,
I find the gentler, subtler
    tones of God.

TAKE ME BACK TO BIMINI

Take me back to Bimini,
to thatched huts, sentinels on sand,
to lazy days where palm tree sways
above the introspective man.

Take me back to Bimini,
to tall, cool drinks and loosened tongues,
to ocean roar which claims no more
than comfort for the aged and young.

Take me back to Bimini,
to golden sands where footprints stay
in moment born and then are gone
replete to wash one's cares away.

ISLAND PLACE

I cannot give to you much more
 than what I hold in human store
 of hope and help, of depth and praise,
 of will to be your *Island place:*

Where you can come and be at peace,
 where you can give your thoughts release,
 where you can writhe and swear and feel
 and know I know which thoughts are real.

 Come to me with your spirits low,
 come to me when you wish to know
 that you are man and man needs this,
 your woman's calm, your woman's kiss.

SAND THOUGHTS I AND II

I find it easy to express
The purest thoughts of happiness
When left to meditate once more
In close communion with the shore.

II

So many years...
    for countless years
our minds are spent on mystery;
    this pull, this force,
    this endless joy
that keeps us traveling to the sea.

AT TWILIGHT

So it became a ritual,
  he standing barefoot on the shore
casting out among the waves,
  'till he would tire and cast no more.

Each evening they then set their
  chairs as tide did ebb and current flow;
she quite content, her book in hand,
  to know what only she could know:

As each wave broke upon the beach
  she felt the spell could last as long—
as they believed it would and so...
  they "splendored" in their island song.

GREAT ISAAC

It is thirty years, but I dream some nights
we are anchored off **Great Isaac Light**
with our sails at rest,
moon round and full,
with the wind as warm
as a cloak of wool.

It is thirty years, yet it seems a day
since we left this shore and sailed away
taking dory to beach,
climbing rock plateau,
viewing Parrot fish
in the surf below.

It is thirty years, but they fall as leaves
when I think of a cove with its lush palm trees,
the creak of the wheel
and the magic of night
as we anchored off
Great Isaac Light.

SANCTUARY

"Mostly poems end saying something
(even the unsayable) but they start as the
body's joy, like making love."
                    — *Donald Hall*

As I retreat to poetry, the great unsayable,
                    soft said,
        it blocks all other reckless thought
                    to keep my reason fed
        in wondrous sweep of blessed tide
                    my intellect is opened wide

and each contrary thought immersed
        in holy, purged, explosive verse.

ETERNAL QUERY

Help me understand what life is all about,
do we live to die or die to live?

The waiting specter: bone on bone, white monuments
all crowded on a hill in leafy park where paper flowers fade.

Yet memories will shape entire lives...
fresh, feverish days when love was born.

Sacred to us are sheep clouds, lush sea oats and skies
of Hatteras blue...a hidden grotto, only two would know,

Salty old Cape Cod, Delmonte in the Pines...
"Take me back to Bimini" in hot Calypso beat,

Misty Isle of Skye, the Hebrides, Windjammer soaring
off Great Isaac Light.
All sweet escapes from commonplace to fantasy.

Myriad of books pile high in quest of comprehension.
We probe the ancients for the secret of our being.

Yet if belief should fail for that beyond,
the blending of our souls as half-light falls

cynics say we are a cheated shell, an empty cup
and death has won...I rage at such a thought.

My ashes shall be so disposed...
to travel through eternity with his.

ENIGMA

If I believe there is no meeting after death
then all my being is betrayed,
my every prayer in vain,
for all my spirit is but a portion of his,
we are combined.
I must accept there shall be beauty after earthly pain.

The sweetest, dearest part of all my days
belong to him and him alone.
My soul was linked to his before my life.
How could the God of love, who granted this,
deny our final joy,
to separate my darling from his wife?

Thus I must trust in every promise given,
although so little mortals understand
of how and where we enter into heaven
to live as one within that other land.

BOATS

Returned to where the waves no longer toss
our boats upon the raging, windy sea,

to calmer waters where we both can share
the beauty of such happy memory.

Now, most content to nestle at the shore,
to rock and creak a bit as evening nears,

we take our ease to contemplate ourselves,
knowing the whisper," thank you God",
                                    He hears.

GOLDEN SUMMER

Oh' summer days of bloom and balm,
Sweet sense of wind and warm.
Recurrent dreams upon a lawn
Of roses... with fat bees all a' swarm.
Oh' languid days of doves in twos
As hummingbird pulled nectar swill,
Where vinca smothered summer's fuse
And lightning strikes consumed the hill.

To celebrate our evening breeze,
To glory in what love repays
We both searched inward then to please
This golden summer of our days.

Ignite that fire! Though there abide one ember,
I shall rake coals...determined to remember.

SMALL WONDER

It is only January on this
                    island in the sea
and I have just discovered
                    Johnny Jump-up's
                    growing free
here in my wind swept garden
as I pull away dead weeds.

It has made this day quite happy:
...such simple joys one needs.

WINGS

"then striving on to meet the sun
his wings were melted by its heat;"

Contemplating the wonderful endeavor of the
Wright Brothers...

ICARUS

Once long ago when earth was young
and men has never dreamed of flight,
Icarus, but a fair hair youth
wondered long at the graceful sight
of gulls who never seemed to tire
or cease to move their wings of white.

With feather of gull and sealing wax
a pair of wings for man, begun
and finished with youth's eagerness;
then striving on to meet the sun
his wings were melted by its heat,
he fell to earth, his dreams undone.

Yet, still he did attempt to fly
to towering heights on untried wings
and so may we our goals attain
by flying on to higher things
to find within each new success
the joys which only flight can bring.

ONE MYSTERY OF THE SEA

He rises long before the dawn.
He stoops to pull his waders on,
retrieves a roll from the bakery bag,
to his belt he ties a fishing rag.

He grabs his pail, his spike and rod,
then takes the path that others trod,
over the dune and through the sand
to claim his spot, his piece of·land.

He baits the hooks, then cast them far
and winks farewell to the morning star.
All worries fade, there is no stress…
   For this, by God, is happiness.

I READ TO WRITE

I read to write, then write to read.
Words fill all impulse of my need.
Some fleeting thought, a naked phrase
can feed full flavor of my days.
Quite chance perceptions seem to flow
to memories that gnaw and grow
until the lines take shape to fill
a living stanza fierce with will.

Could such a craft make time the pawn
to fill that span from dusk till dawn
with grand illusion and compete
in every marketplace and street?
I have no answer, yet it seems
that poetry is made of dreams...

MYSTIC – ORACLE

And with each century there appears
these persons out of time and place—
yet feelings bridging all the years,
a questing out of heaven's space
   for man's true meaning, his wish
   to make of this a better land.

A jealous group of fellows we who
poke and prod, then test with fire,
yet care so trifling what they do,
this alchemy of heart's desire;
   the oracle, his gift so free,
   his wisdom just beyond our gate.

How time has proved these chosen ones.
We only look to history
   to find all but too late that man
   has overlooked their mystery!

WINGS

A Sonnet

Purple sky, clouds gray, clouds white.
Wings pierce air in measured flight.
Dawn of age, launch of dream,
Glide and soar, slip, careen,
Shoot the moon, play the stars,
Hold that course to include Mars.
Galaxy of growth and gain
While remnants of the fire remain
To kindle faith that flight will be
The showpiece of our century.
Could such a dream that man began
Be entered in eternal plan
And so demand of you and I,
We reach of limits of the sky?

THE THUNDERBOLT

In that reckless crack of light,
  the streak of searing heat...
    a kindling born.

Yet only in one lifetime
  and plainly to the few
    comes such a detonation.

The glance of eye,
  a toss of head, the smile...
    shy omen another soul exists.

Aggregate, this cell of chance
  in life's mad fortune molds our fate,
    predestination, destiny.

Then what has will to do with it at all?
  Can one be seared forever by such jolt,
    harvesting eternally...
              love's thunderbolt?

REMINISCENCE

We save one pure defense as evening falls,
that haunting, poignant laughter of the day
for every one of us who fond recalls
some gracious, gentle time now put away
but filed in memory for later years
when we shall sorely crave it to renew
a brighter, happier respite from our tears...
now neatly shelved and hidden from our view.
How happy we, who tap into that store,
when youth has flown and days are growing small,
to find that sweet remembrance is more
than need sustain us, waiting for the call.
For what remains of this world's tawdry schemes
but memories of our laughter and our dreams?

WHAT MAN CAN DREAM...

What man can dream, then surely he can do.
No boundaries for that quintessential sage,
   propelled by will...and only to a few
   did Intiution lure men of our age.

Could flight be art but of a different sort?
and exploration reprieve from earth's grasp
   in winds that clear the very soul's import
   to God, all settled in and joyful at the task?

Is all flight seeking wider view of life
from heights so unimagined at earth's birth
   in finding certain meaning from the strife
   which man has loosed upon this tragic earth?

Did Orville, Wilbur, join those mystic few,
the children Eos sent at early dawn:
   Boreas, Zephyr, Notus... in elements anew,
   Dauntless to fly their daring dreams upon?

GLIDER PILOT

Soundless as a world wraps tight around.
Breathless in pure opulence, new found.
Fearless as smooth air currents astound.
Carefree in my loss of mortal sound.

What gives to one this need to fly
and reach that domain of some sky,
to glide and soar, to dip and bow,
to feel this lightness, I know now?

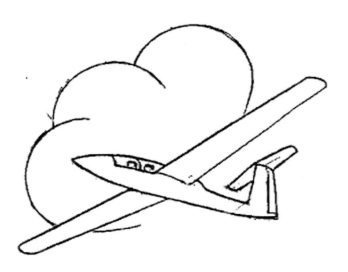

PRAYER ON A DARK DAY

Please, God, the journey is so long
and I am tired of travel.
My baggage carried, burdensome—
so I cannot unravel
all the twists and turns of stress
in roads that lead to happiness…

My feet are sore, my mouth is dry.
I long for manna from some sky and
lust for entry where my cry be heard.

I sense no end in sight, you see,
and only black envelopes me.
Please give me strength to move away
from this relentless, darkest day.

"the supreme fiction" Wallace Stevens
or "my craft and sullen art" Dylan Thomas

If poetry would be the all, the great equality of soul,
then I have wealth beyond its' toll and kind reprieve
                              from mortal goal.

If lyric text releases me, speaking incessant in my brain,
I seek no succor to life's pain, but welcome verse
                              as summer's rain.

Believe the lyricist, in truth, his ear does hear another beat;
he captures that which makes life sweet and writes to
                              prove his world complete.

UNBOUNDED SPIRAL

Again a bird has risen from the nest.
His wings seem lighter than the air he tries.
Once more he soars up higher than the rest
Of earthly ramparts, reaching for the skies.
Observe the ease, the majesty and grace:
No thing can match such effort on the ground.
This entity is celebrating space,
Apparent in some secret it has found.
As man has met this marvel, newly gained
That nature had decreed since ancient time,
His affirmation surely is proclaimed
In certain art he's contrived to refine.
Unbounded spirit, can such skill be pure?
Will man be soaring when but birds endure?

WEED WORDS

At first there only fell one word,
a sour sound, but light and thin,
yet time recalled it as a blow
with bitter memory cased therein.
In tension then grim anguished days
spilled over as a rushing brook
and gall re-visited in thought
creating anger as she took
her malice to begin a void,
an aching place want could not fill...
so hatred grew...oh' dearest heart
when only one small word went ill...
yes, hatred grew with wretched speed
and only one small word the seed.

ICARUS ASCENDING

In myth, might it be fair to say
that fifty years is like a day
and Icarus was skyward bound
in testing out those wings he found
for eons, like some child at play.

On earth could it be just the same
for mortals in that search for fame
or peace, or love or happiness,
who struggle nonstop in caress
of vast endeavor with no name?

I feel beyond this veil of clay,
sweeping all dust of time away,
there must be life unending,
and in some dream, revealed one day,
we'll apprehend...Icarus ascending.

SOUNDINGS

*"skimmers sweep with added grace upon
our channel to retrieve their prizes won?"*

POET – NOUVEAU RICHE

Who needs the sounds of poets anymore?
Will flowers smell more sweetly at the door?
Or skimmers sweep with added grace upon
Our channel to retrieve their prizes won?
Who needs the voice to complement his own:
Will life take on a richer, rosy hue
If one is pointed to a value known
To make us conscious of life's "postage due?"
We each within this flesh and matter gray
Are well equipped to sort and sense and feel
Yet hardened by the grind of everyday
We hide our finest thoughts, deny the real;
The love, the hope and faith we might restore-
Who needs the sounds of poets anymore?

TO MNEMOSYNE, GODDESS OF MEMORY

If memory stays
the spirit lives
and time will build a treasure store
with rows and shelves, with bins and such
for nights when old age pounds the door.

Then heartaches ease,
contentment dwells
for those who quite forget their pain
but reach into a bag of tricks
to draw sweet memories back again.

THE VERNAL SEASON

The month was May, the season, spring.
Bright sun exploded amid trees
on two who shared the magic of the park.
It was a morning meant for only love
and proved to be the prelude to one kiss.
Could any act on earth be held as tender?

Dark haired and curly headed, he, intensely tender
sensed all the lovely wonderment of spring.
His hesitation …honoring that kiss
was only first imagined, whispered in the trees,
then in that rapture called first love
the couple felt alone within the park.

All other ears were sealed, muffled in this park
to murmured words of sweetness, oh, so tender.
Deep feelings swelled, excitement turned to love
as gods gazed down through endless springs
when even birds who nestle in the trees
seem shy to view a first and gentle kiss.

That kiss, sweet kiss, it scarce be called a kiss
for close beside a bridge, within the park
the wind had blown about through leafy trees
to catch her soft brown hair in tangled tenders
since this was in the early flush of spring,
a whisper touch to a brow all brimmed in love.

Please picture this, ours was truly love.
and sixty years has not erased that kiss.
Each year the anniversary of our spring
makes me reminiscent of the park,
of a precious kiss to my temple, so tender,

where only those to view it were the trees.

I shall be ever grateful to those trees,
they shaded us encircling safe our love.
They hold the wealth of memories, all tender,
for when I close my eyes, I feel that blessed kiss
and long for one small moment in the park
to capture briefly our first rite of spring.

What does one hold when life has flown but this:
permitting tender kisses in a park of tree filled spring,
perceiving purest music...of forever love.

WOMAN

God gave me a eye to see His beauty
and a mouth to kiss a man.

God gave me an ear to hear His love song
and a mind to know His plan.

I am the instrument of His love.
I am the hope for time to be.

God gave me a soul to keep His logic
then a heart to set it free.

God gave me the gift to write with power
and to make men try for grace.

God gave me a voice to shout injustice
and a love to fill its place.

I am the instrument of His love.
I am the hope for time to be.

I am WOMAN holding vigil.
I am keeper of the key.

THE BURNING

If in each life... could come one time
        to STOP it all
for those few weeks when shock subsides,
then drugs withdraw and pain begins

and pain exists and pain consumes
        and pain controls,
yet in that sweet, exquisite pain, the mind
        renews all fresh to earth's allure.

Could one be bold to start again,
just as the flesh has started too,
in drawing up, in pulling in,
in hardening over all the sore,
the red and raw with delicate
new veil of flesh...
        as virgin as a blade of grass?

If in each life there could but be one burning!

I SHOULD CONVEY

I should convey some modest thoughts
　　of lazy, languid afternoons
　　　　when time ticked free
　　　　　　and openly
　　the house held heavy with perfumes

of roasted beef and thickened smell
　　of apples cooking long and sweet,
　　　　the peaceful drone ·
　　　　　　of telephone
　　with plans to make the day complete.

Our Sunday took on such a feel, a joyful
　　gentle truth in time
　　　　when simple pleasure
　　　　　　grew from treasure
　　knowledge of our clan design.

In memory do days grow sweet
　　and only happy times occur
　　　　to push our thought
　　　　　　in ways that ought
　　make just the pleasant ones endure?

DEVISED

Separation is to some
   a much sought respite,
   planned and earned,
while others tolerate its course
   with small annoyance.
   factor learned!

Do not divorce my eyes from yours,
your hand from mine to hold.
Oh' do not take your warmth away
to let my soul grow cold.

One day without your tenderness
is summer without sun.
A weekend when our lips don't touch,
an eclipse has begun.

WISHES

"if turnips were watches"
—Mother Goose

Near sixty-five,...so much to do,
I would that I were twenty-two:

The book to write, the shop to own,
A world to view, dull knives to hone,
A bareback rider, trainer of seals,
The joker perched upon high wheels,
Builder of bridges, a chimney sweep,
A diver in the sea so deep,
A vineyard master, sipping wine,
The peasant picking from the vine,
A soda jerk, a circus clown,
The one who knocks tall buildings down,
A mountain climber, man's pure confessor,
A whiz on the latest work processor,
A pastry chef with a wedding cake,
A flutist charming mystic snake,
The gambler showing how to deal,
A farmer calming pig's high squeal,
A minister, a movie star,
The stunt man in his racing car,
A pickle seller on the street,
The doctor easing aching feet,
A researcher who finds the cure,
Xylophone teacher, chaste and pure,
An ice-cream manufacturer...oh'

All these I'd be and many more...
If I were not now sixty-four.

SONNET OF DAVID'S 7TH PSALM

Oh' Lord, my God, in thee I put my trust.
Save me from persecution for I must
Keep wickedness forever from my hand
Or let my enemies turn honor into sand.
The Lord shall judge His people, judge me now
According to the innocence in me.
Oh' righteous God, be patient and allow
This servant who provokes you so to be
Child of a patient judge, true of heart,
Not conceived in mischief or untruth,
Not fallen to distrust, but set apart and
Held to keep the wisdom of his youth.
I thank the Lord according to His right
And praise the name of God with all my might.

REMEMBER

If words could recall some feeling,
That dear innocence of youth,
The filmy feel of a fabric
Or a sweet as it touched the tooth;
If we speak to convey a humor
That floats in vaporous air
As the gentle breeze wafts through it
And is tumbled in our hair...
Then our words might recapture feelings
And the pleasure that is sent
For the great delight of memory
Is the sweetest sentiment.

Yes, the treasure of our memory
Is what we never shall forget.

THE PRUNERS

Poetry of the Italian Soul

Ancient and gnarled as the limbs they prune,
   dutifully, two pay homage to one more spring,
connected to the other, as tree to branch,
   in union, encircled by a wedding ring.

Forsaking wintry chills and released to feel
   a thermal sun pull through antique bone,
voiceless, they sense this might be the time
   that could leave one to trim vines alone.

Yet should the fates permit this plight,
   if such a destined day be looming,
then each will bless that vast godsend
   for granting…lovely years of pruning.

WE ARE ALWAYS LEAVING SOMETHING

Much is made of the petty stores we hoard,
yet is there not a more important gain?
That gentle, softer art of leaving something
evokes much joy, but equally, acute, exquisite pain.
Long before our earliest recollection
we leave our mother's womb to know the world,
we leave our father's hand to try first steps,
then parting from the warm cocoon they ruled-
we cling to others who instruct, prepare and mold.

We move to schools, leaving friends behind, though
in such partings, sweet, fine words are measured.
We leave positions, leave good neighbors too
plus books, belongings we had counted treasure.
Then in the mad, mad world of daily being,
we leave more mundane items such as these:
umbrellas left in restaurants or on buses,
old hats, our reading glasses and our keys.

We are always leaving something:
a lover for some reason, never sure,
the child with promise of our swift return,
that bittersweet, deep yearning for the pure.
We leave our childhood hopes, the fantasies,
those great imaginings which prompted dreams.
We leave a fairytale existence that is joy
and leaving enter what the world terms schemes.

Yet, leaving is the grandest thing we do.
It takes possession of our very soul.
That grace in which we choose the way to leave
holds volumes of our character and so—
as all is winding down and days grow small

with creature comforts needed, close at hand,
we sit and ponder various times in life
when leaving something proved the happy land.

For now as our full measure must be told,
we trust in what is honest and is true:
this leaving something of ourselves is all
we have to give…

                    to you, my dears, to you.

LOVES LOST

Loves lost are not to say they never were.
The aching pain of just remembering,
makes every fiber of my being stir
to some forgotten semblance of spring
when bird was nesting, buds burst full to bloom,
a special lightness captivating sense,
imaginings surge forward like perfume,
awakenings recur with no defense.
Would it be better that these feelings cease,
this unrequited passion for the past,
the stinging, burning that our thoughts release
thrusting us sharply back in dies long cast?
Would life be sweeter without bonds star-crossed
reliving memories of our lovers lost?

WRITING

Begin, begin the pen...the hand,
    a foreign force in foreign land.

The soul can tell in trillion beat
    those words that leave the page effete.

Deep anguish pours...wide open ache
    and the heart keeps still
                for writing sake.

POETRY

Poetry is the hope of the world.
It makes us feel...as nothing else on earth can do.
It opens up the mind, the heart, to truths impossible
                to sense in any other way.

Poetry is the soul of the world.
It gives us the power to wish to do good.
It creates in us the will to be just.
It grants us a peace to be found in no other emissary.

Poetry is a power all to itself.
When I am sorrowful, I turn expectantly to it.
When I have boundless joy, it is my true companion.
My life would be merely a shell without poetry.

AUTUMN SONG

Nothing quite so plaintive,
Nothing quite so sad
    As when leaves fall in cadence
    To the memories we had
    Of sweet, small children twisting,
    Straining, laughing in the dusk,
    Of wood smoke curling skyward
    On an apple cider musk.

Nothing to touch heart strings
    Or pull the senses keen
    As soft, melancholy music
    Of the cool, nocturnal stream
    Rippling aestivel magic,
    Retracing adolescent dream.

So there are none to be ecstatic
    When the skimmer, dipping low,
    Sees his own reflection mirrored,
    Turned from ways he meant to go…
    Now, before the autumn holds us
    We rush headlong into snow.

COMING HOME

They say that not by deed or pen
may we presume "to go home again."

Those long remembered flawless dreams
which now sustain our current schemes
lie just beneath the conscious mind,
leaving more modest thoughts behind.

Yet born to each are peaceful days
of lost, enchanted, lovely ways
when parents held the child, proud,
as gentle words were voiced aloud.
For through a miracle of time
our hearts recall those days sublime;
the walks through woods, of sandy shore,
of fables read, we hear no more.

We each, within such happenstance,
are blessed with this remembrance.
Though never tangibly attained
in reminiscence we've proclaimed
to find no matter where we roam...
in spirit,... we are "Coming home".

SANDCASTLES

"He leads her and she follows fast,,
she leaps, he feels her wake,"

TWO

Just barely seen from the distant shore
   two shapes which rise and fall
   and we're scarcely sure with the ocean's roar
   that they're really there at all.

He leads her and she follows fast,
   she leaps, he feels her wake
   and so attune is each at last
   they sense how each wave breaks.

So over the years as the two rejoice
   in the dash and spume of the crest
   they each can hear that inner voice
   calling, "this has been life's best."

LISTEN, LISTEN...

Now all our days
pass by too fast,
to catch their fragrance
to the last,
to hold each precious
blissful time
your head has lain
so close to mine.

Hold still these days,
these hours of love,
'till I would speak
to you and prove
my everlasting
need of you
before these lovely
days are through...

FABRIC

I want

to lay my soul so bare
the threads will show,
to open up the weave
so you will know
the inner meshing of
my heart and mind.

I cannot

open wide enough to you,
to make you feel this
happiness I am
when you are near me.

ONLY TRUE JOY...

Only true joy when
beauty is shared,
otherwise we become
ever impaired
by guarding our secrets,
hoarding our gold
keeping each eye away
as we grow old.

Only true joy when
we can give pleasure
is love's lesson learned,
as life's greatest treasure
must never be hidden,
the gift is to give
for only by sharing
will we know we have lived.

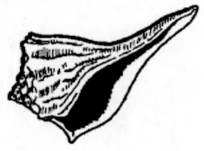

AUGMENTATION

Perhaps a love should always stay
    just as it first began
and never change intensity
    as part of one great plan,
and it that's true as it may be
    then something's surely wrong with me.

For everyday in everyway
    I love you more and more.
You cannot even comprehend
    the way that I adore
your every action and the smile
    that truly makes my life worthwhile.

So whether I am right or wrong
    I really do not care.
I'll just go right on loving you
    and live this love we share,
then let the love which wants to so
    just grow and grow and grow and grow!

ANALYST

When all is said and done,
  then what is love,
  a meeting of two minds,
  companionship,
  two hearts conceding
  they exist as one?

Who is to say they
  can define the word,
  for love to one may
  mean a tempered life,
  and to another,
  rapt, consuming fire.

It lies within the heart
  for each to find.
  While some would search
  the world and all in vain,
  I've found all love,
  all life within your kiss.

50's

So comfortable, this thing they share,
  he soundless in his easy chair,
  no urgent love words to declare,
  just conscious of her being there.

All calm and peaceful flow the days,
  she ever mindful of his praise
  yet knowing what his smile betrays
  in subtle, sensuous interplays.

Grown to look and think as one,
  effortless as morning sun,
  in laughter and sorrow, this pact begun
  as partners...till their day is done.

COMMUNICATION

I say just what there is to say
   in short, clipped sentences of need.

In longer speech I list my goals,
   articulate my creed.

A hot impassioned verbal swell
   denotes the import of my rage,

Soft, sympathetic tones impart
   what only grief can gauge.

Our voice is used in countless ways
to sort the intent of our days
and when a word is out of reach
we curse that limit of our speech.

TOUCHING

I believe in touching:

The warmth of your hand
   pressed hard on mine,
The touch of lips on hair,
   a gentle touch,

The way you touch my arm
   to guide or lead...
and the most beautiful touch
   of lips in

Hello

or

Goodbye

or just in happy together.

GIFT

One day upon another builds
   in endless, block like stratosphere
and we are put a portion of
   the ever-changing present, here.

But if we love as lovers should
   and give to each the need to be,
then all has been in balance as
   I live in you ...and you in me.

MARRIAGE – 33RD YEAR

You lie beside me
deeply now in sleep
encumbered by the
care to which you'll wake.
I lie here listening
to you breathe,
content to know the
difference that I make
       in loving you. ·

       Twelve thousand days
       like this...
       with only God to say
       how many more.
       Count only that I'd
       live them all again.
       Count only that the
       what I'm living for
          Is loving you.

THE STORY LADY

Bedtime for Ali...eight years old.

The story lady comes before I sleep
and sits beside my bed to hold my hand.
She tell me of a place where fairies leap
from one tremendous mountain to the sand,
of castles where a princess dressed in silk
sips honey nectar from a golden cup,
where elves and gnomes turn water into milk
and make a hundred kittens lap it up.

The story lady sings before she goes,
a soft sweet song and every night the same.
She pats my hand and bundles in my toes
and never, ever lets me know her name.
One day when I am very grown and tall
I want to softly cross that shaft of light
to sing and dream to children of my own
and be their story lady of the night.

HERMITAGE

The images are strong and clear,
remembrance is sweeter dear
    perhaps than even on the day
    when first I gave my love away.

No human hand can ever take
this bittersweet and lovely ache
    from here within my secret sighs
    or steal the memory of your eyes.

CONSTANCY

Hold tight my hand
when night begins to lengthen.
Cradle me within the hollow
                of your arm.

My dreams are sweet,
my pulses throb and strengthen.
I feel a peace that cannot
                know alarm.

Hold firm my waist,
encircle me with your love.
Let breath on breath say all
                we wish to hear.

So let it prove...
one night upon another,
until our breath shall cease
                and leave us here.

PORTENT

At times it feels that there exists
only the flutter of a brow
or but a single day between that
time when I was just thirteen and now.

At sixty-three, it seems to me
I wish all younger poets to sense
how time will fly in twinkling eye
before their final recompense.

Be stringent with the written word,
make every phrase and dream ring true,
for fifty years is but the muse
insuring what endures of you.

VILLA

Poetry of the Italian Soul

The Kitchen

Peasant odors, too complex to explain,
Float on air all warm with spice and sweet.
Pots shine upon the range as they proclaim
A holy, ancient ritual, complete
With sausage, peppers, oregano and cheese,
Polenta, pasta, eggs and fragrant bread.
These basics of my villa kitchen please
The master of our house some hours ahead
Of midday, when this glory will combine
Our sensual selves in Epicurean need:
This earthy, noble sustenance to bind
Our hunger with such energy to feed
These sunny days, all-resolute in beams
Of love, filling our *cucina* with aromatic dreams.

VILLA

Poetry of the Italian Soul

The Balcony

I rest against the doorjamb of delight
Subscribing to a breeze that flows to free
My sensual self in seasons of the night
From all the pulsing rhythms of the sea.
Then warm on warm our bodies' stretched to cool
As hovering gulls swept close to view the tryst.
And tepid tiles beneath marked evening duel
For bargains where realities exist in
Every breath of sweetly whispered word.
This fragile fairytale, reinforced in bliss,
Would recognize all cares of life, absurd.
When he bestowed that perfect, measured kiss
Our villa world was but one sigh apart
From heaven… days now sacred to my heart.

VILLA

Poetry of the Italian Soul

Sun Porch

His hands so perfect in the way they moved,
So perfect in the beauty that they wrought.
Those hands so wired to mind and proved
Through every carved complexity, his thought.
Sun porch all filled with rays to light his soul,
A room he occupied for hours on end,
This fitting sunspace to complete his goal
Of marvelous design and charming, sweet pretend.
Those endless moments spent in such a place
Seemed to warm his inner -self as well.
The beauty he created in that space
Remains to mark a greatness and will tell
His intellect… as it will long remind us of
My sun porch man, genius of extraordinary kind

THE TEARS OF THINGS

... Virgil

What moves the soul to wonder,
        to reverence and release,
What gives my eye its pleasure
        and imagery of peace?
I cannot now remember
        how I came to tarry here,
How warm it seemed, that curving
        from all outward worldly fear
As waters, soft, washed over
        and sweet rivers rushed to swell,
Proving all my troubles hollow
        as the sounding of a bell.
Surely exaltation leads me,
        call it fate or chance or will,
Soundly there are paths to follow
        even through the forest - still
With every twist and hanging,
        every gnarled branch and limb
Bright, pure light astounds the clearing,
        splashing hope to cups' full brim.

What moves the soul to wonder,
        to emotion, happiness?
Is a silent force now working
        in some place we can but guess?
Could entire worlds be forming
        while celestial choirs sing
As our joys are mounting, mounting...
        within the *tears of things?*

About the author…

Doris Dix Caruso, born in Oak Park and educated in Chicago, Illinois, has written poetry all of her life.

In 1974 she and her husband, Adolph, moved to the outer banks of North Carolina on Cape Hatteras, to live in their "villa" and to take pleasure in the beauty and peace of the beaches there.

Doris now lives in the pleasant Piedmont portion of North Carolina where she continues to write both novels and poetry.

Her works have appeared in literary journals, Chicago magazines and poetry annuals.

****

Copies of this volume can be obtained
        by mailing $11.50 (price includes postage)

    To:

        SEASHORE JOURNALS
        Doris Dix Caruso
        146 West Crescent Square Drive,
        Graham, NC 27253